Genre › Myth

Essential Question
Why do people tell and retell myths?

Thor's Journey to Utgard

BY JAMES McNAUGHTON
ILLUSTRATED BY JARED OSTERHOLD

Chapter 1
The Giant 2

Chapter 2
Utgard 6

Chapter 3
More Challenges 10

Chapter 4
The Truth Is Revealed 13

Respond to Reading 16

PAIRED READ Thor's Counselor 17

Focus on Genre 20

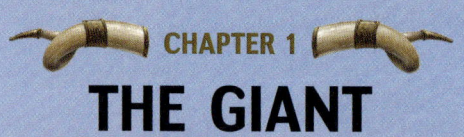

CHAPTER 1
THE GIANT

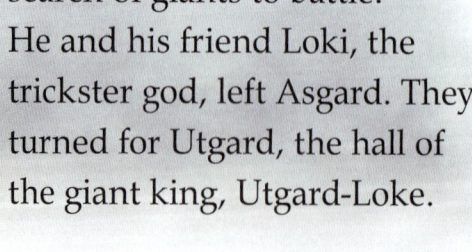

Thor was the greatest fighter of all the gods in Asgard. The blows of his magic hammer, Mjollnir, created thunder and lightning across the heavens.

One day, Thor went in search of giants to battle. He and his friend Loki, the trickster god, left Asgard. They turned for Utgard, the hall of the giant king, Utgard-Loke.

Thor and Loki walked all day, and as night fell, they approached a forest. The trees were so tall that their tops disappeared into the clouds. They had reached Giant Land.

The two friends entered a strange building with four narrow rooms and a larger side chamber. Lying down in the longest room, they soon fell asleep.

In the middle of the night, an earthquake awoke them. The building shook, and there was a **dreadful** rumbling sound. Thor and Loki crept into the side chamber, and Thor stood guard with his hammer.

After hours of wind, noise, and shaking, Thor decided he'd had enough. He strode into the forest. There he found a giant, fast asleep. The giant's snores were making the ground shake and the forest tremble.

Thor grasped his hammer and struck a blow on the giant's head. The giant opened one enormous eye and mumbled, "Hmm, a leaf must have landed on me." His eye closed, and he went back to sleep.

STOP AND CHECK

Why did Thor and Loki leave their home?

Thor was angry. He gathered all his strength, took a running leap, and swung his mightiest blow.

This time the giant grumbled and sat up. Rubbing his head, he looked up in the branches. He said to himself, "A bird must have knocked a piece of moss down from the tree." Then, he looked down and saw Thor.

"Good morning!" Thor said. "May I ask your name?"

CHAPTER 2
UTGARD

"My name is Skrymir," he said. "You must be Thor. I've heard of your **exploits**." Looking around, he said, "I've lost a glove. Ah, there it is." He reached for the funny looking building that Thor and Loki had slept in. It was the giant's glove! The four rooms were for his fingers, and the side chamber for his thumb.

Thor called out, "Wait!" He raced into the glove to wake up Loki.

After Loki had introduced himself, they told Skrymir they were bound for Utgard.

"In Utgard," said Skrymir, "many men are as tall as I am. Keep quiet when you arrive. They dislike **boasting**." Then Skrymir said goodbye and strode away.

When Thor and Loki arrived at Utgard, they went to the hall of the giant king, Utgard-Loke. The massive hall was a forbidding sight. The rumbling voices and bursts of laughter coming from within sounded **fearsome**. However, Thor and Loki were **valiant** gods, so they entered.

Inside the hall a group of massive giants sat at two long tables. The two gods approached the king, Utgard-Loke. They introduced themselves.

Utgard-Loke smiled scornfully and said, "Little fellows, you have much **audacity** to come here. You might be gods, but I'm not convinced. If you prove you are good at something, I will allow you to remain here."

Loki stepped forward. "I can eat faster than anyone. Does anyone here have the courage to compete against me?"

Utgard-Loke laughed at the little god. "If you can beat our champion eater, I will be impressed!"

A giant stomped forward. A long wooden **trough** filled with meat was set on the floor.

"Start at opposite ends," said Utgard-Loke to Loki and the giant. "The first one to eat his way to the middle will be the winner. Go!"

Loki started at one end, and the giant at the other. The giants shouted and stamped their feet while the two ate.

Loki ate furiously, using both hands. The giant was casual, rather delicately using only his thumb and forefinger. Within minutes, they met in the middle of the trough. But while Loki had eaten only the meat, the giant had eaten the bones and trough as well.

The giants declared Loki the loser.

> **STOP AND CHECK**
>
> Why did Loki compete in an eating contest?

CHAPTER 3
MORE CHALLENGES

Utgard-Loke peered down at Thor and said, "Are you good at anything?"

Thor answered, "I'm known for my mighty thirst. I can drink mountain streams dry."

Utgard-Loke handed Thor a drinking horn brimming with water. "A good drinker can empty this horn in one drink," he said. "An average drinker in two, and a weak drinker in three."

Thor took a huge breath and drank and drank, but the water level hardly changed.

The giants began to bang their fists on the tables.

Thor took a deep breath and drank again. Finally, with his breath exploding from his lungs, he set the horn down.

"At least the horn can now be carried without spilling," laughed Utgard-Loke.

The giants roared with laughter.

"Try something easier," said Utgard-Loke. He gestured to his cat, which was asleep at his feet. "Why don't you try lifting this cat?"

Thor bent down and went to lift up the cat. It was surprisingly heavy. Thor applied all his strength, but the cat didn't budge. With a great heave, Thor tried again. Finally a paw lifted off the ground, but a second later it dropped back to the ground.

Angry, Thor yelled, "I can wrestle anyone!"

"My old nurse, Eli, would make a good match," said Utgard-Loke. "Bring her in!"

A skinny old woman shuffled into the hall. Thor was embarrassed at the sight of her. He extended his hand in a friendly gesture, and at once found himself on his back at the other side of the hall. The old woman cackled, and the giants howled with laughter.

Thor lunged for Eli. Locked together in a wrestlers' hold, each searched for a point of weakness. An hour went by. Thor finally got her in a headlock, but she twisted out of it with explosive power. The giants **jeered** at Thor.

"Stop," called Utgard-Loke. "We need to eat dinner. But let me just say this, Thor. I don't think you should challenge anyone else."

Thor and Loki remained quiet and **somber** for the rest of the night, despite being given plenty to eat.

STOP AND CHECK

Why did Thor fight Eli?

CHAPTER 4
THE TRUTH IS REVEALED

The next morning, Thor and Loki were preparing to leave when Utgard-Loke appeared in their chambers. He insisted they eat breakfast with him.

After breakfast, Utgard-Loke led them out through the city gates. The giant crouched down to speak with his guests. He asked, "How did you enjoy your journey to Utgard?"

"I am ashamed," Thor replied sadly. "You must think poorly of me."

"Not at all. If I'd known you were so **steadfast**," Utgard-Loke said, "I would never have allowed you to enter Utgard in the first place."

"But Loki and I failed every challenge!"

"I will tell you the truth," said Utgard-Loke. "But only if you promise never to return."

Thor nodded his head in agreement.

STOP AND CHECK

Why did Thor feel ashamed?

"Thor, I practiced the art of **deception** on you," said Utgard-Loke.

"First, I disguised myself as the giant Skrymir. You believed you were striking his head with your hammer, but you were really hitting a mountain. It now has deep valleys."

The giant continued. "In each of the contests, I used magic. You were both **oblivious** to what was really happening. The giant who beat Loki was actually Fire, who consumes everything." Loki was astonished.

Utgard-Loke continued. "Thor, that drinking horn extended to the sea. Your drinking set the sea in motion."

Stunned, Thor asked, "And what of the cat?"

"The cat was actually the Midgard Serpent."

Thor shook his head. "That little cat was the serpent that encircles the world?" he asked.

"Yes. You nearly pulled its tail out of its mouth," answered Utgard-Loke.

Thor was amazed. "And the old woman Eli?"

"Eli is Old Age, whom no one will ever defeat. The way you wrestled her was **astounding**."

Utgard-Loke could see that his deception had caused Thor great anger. He said, "Now you must keep your promise. Leave and never return."

Thor did not want to let the king of the giants get away with such trickery.

Angry, Thor swung his hammer, but it passed through thin air. Utgard-Loke had disappeared, and so had the city, its walls, and all the other giants. The two friends stood on a **desolate** plain.

Respond to Reading

Summarize

Use details from the myth to summarize *Thor's Journey to Utgard*. Your graphic organizer may help you.

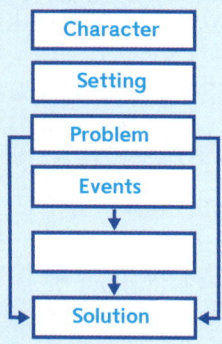

Text Evidence

1. What is one of Thor's problems after he reaches Utgard? How is it solved? **PROBLEM AND SOLUTION**

2. Find the word *forbidding* on page 7. What clues help you to understand the word's meaning? **VOCABULARY**

3. Write about the problem Thor and Loki have in Chapter 1. How does Thor try to solve it? **WRITE ABOUT READING**

Genre > **Parody**

Compare Texts
Read an updated myth about how Thor tames his anger.

THOR'S COUNSELOR

Thor wanted to go to Utgard to battle giants. He wanted to hurl his magic hammer, creating thunder and lightning as giants toppled like trees.

Thor suggested this plan to his anger management counselor.

"We've moved on from this destructive behavior," his counselor said. "Let's simply pay the giants in Utgard a friendly visit. I'll pack some vegetarian meals and come along."

"Yes, of course," said Thor with a sigh. He knew he couldn't just go out and beat up giants anymore. Discouraged, he walked along the walls of Asgard while his counselor prepared salads to take with them.

Before they set off, Thor agreed to use his hammer, Mjollnir, for self defense only.

That night, they took shelter in a hut. Before long, a roaring and whistling noise awoke them. Thor leaped up, ready for a fight.

"That sounds like a giant with a snoring problem," said the counselor. "We'll let him sleep."

Thor gripped his hammer. He repeated to himself, "Violence is not the answer."

Upon arriving in Utgard, they met the king of the giants, Utgard-Loke. He challenged Thor to prove himself in a contest.

"I challenge anyone to a fight!" Thor exclaimed.

"No," said his counselor. "How about a dancing contest?"

The giants considered this.

"I prefer eating to dancing," said Utgard-Loke. He pointed to pigs roasting on spits at the far end of the hall.

Thor's mouth began watering like a mountain stream. "What a fine idea!"

"Thor, here's your salad," the counselor reminded him.

Thor's heart sank.

"Good for you, Thor," said Utgard-Loke, trying to cheer him up. "You're in much better shape than I am."

"Thanks," answered Thor. It was the first compliment a giant had ever given him. "I like the workmanship on your gates," he said.

And so Thor, his counselor, and the giants had a pleasant conversation about the work of craftsmen and artisans. Thor left Utgard the next morning, but he was invited to come back whenever he felt like getting out of Asgard.

Make Connections

Why might the character of Thor appeal to storytellers and listeners time after time?
ESSENTIAL QUESTION

Compare the endings of both selections. What is different? TEXT TO TEXT

Focus on Genre

Myth Myths are a form of folk stories. They usually tell about gods or heroic figures. Sometimes they explain things that happen in the natural world. Myths come from many different cultures. They often have characters with supernatural powers. They usually take place long ago, when the world was different from how it is today.

Read and Find In *Thor's Journey to Utgard*, Thor is a god who has supernatural powers. He can drink mountain streams dry and make thunder and lightning with his hammer.

Your Turn

Work with a partner or small group. Reread *Thor's Journey to Utgard*. Discuss the following questions.

Who is a hero in this myth? What clues can you find about a character who meets a challenge or solves a problem?

How is the setting of this myth different from the world today?

What events in the natural world does this myth explain?